Folk Songs
of the
West Country

Folk Songs of the West Country

Collected by
Sabine Baring-Gould

Annotated from the MSS at Plymouth Library and with
additional material by Gordon Hitchcock

B780·24

DAVID & CHARLES
NEWTON ABBOT   LONDON   NORTH POMFRET (VT)   VANCOUVER
KEITH PROWSE MUSIC PUBLISHING CO LTD

To Pat Shaw

0 7153 6419 7

© Gordon Hitchcock 1974

All rights reserved. No part of this publication may be reproduced, stored in a retrieval system, or transmitted, in any form or by any means, electronic, mechanical, photocopying, recording or otherwise, without the prior permission of David & Charles (Holdings) Limited

Published in the United States of America
by David & Charles Inc
North Pomfret Vermont 05053 USA

Published in Canada
by Douglas David & Charles Limited
3645 McKechnie Drive West Vancouver BC

Set in Times Roman
by Avontype (Bristol) Limited
and printed in Great Britain by
Biddles Limited, Guildford
for David & Charles (Holdings) Limited
South Devon House Newton Abbot Devon

Contents

Foreword	7
Adieu to Old England	10
A-hunting We Will Go	12
As I Walked Out	14
Banks of Sweet Primeroses	16
Bonny Blue Handkerchief	18
Carpenter's Wife, The	20
Chase the Buffalo	22
Coasts of Barbary	24
Come All You Worthy Christian Men	26
Come, My Lads	28
Constant Johnny	30
Cuckoo	32
Emigrant's Song	34
Evening Prayer	36
Flora, Lily of the West	38
Foolish Boy, The	40
Forsaken Maiden, The	42
Golden Vanity, The	44
Green Besoms	46
Green Cockade, The	48
Greenland Whale Fishery	50
Henry Martyn	52
Her Contented Farmer's Son	54
Highwayman	56
Hostess's Daughter	58
In Bibberly Town	60
In Bodmin Town	62
I Rode My Little Horse	64
Jinny Jan	66
Jolly Waggoner	68
Lark in the Morn, The	70
Lark in the Morning	72
Lying Tale, A	74
Maids at Eighteen	76
Months of the Year	78
O the Sweet Streams of Nancy	80
Owl, The	82
Ploughboys' Song	84
Poor Old Horse	86
Rich Nobleman	88
Rosemary Lane	90
Roving Journeyman	92
Saucy Sailor	94
Deep in Love	96
Sweet Nightingale	98
Twankidillo	100
Twelve Days of Christmas	102
Wassail Song	104
Widdecombe Fair	106
Wreck off Scilly, The	108
Sabine Baring-Gould: A Memoir	110

Alternative Titles

A-Roving, *see* Jolly Waggoner
A-Nutting We Will Go, *see* A-hunting We Will Go
Beverley Maid, The, *see* In Bibberly Town
Don't Let Me Die an Old Maid, *see* Maids at Eighteen
I'm Seventeen Come Sunday, *see* As I Walked Out
False-hearted Knight, *see* Rich Nobleman
Jenny Jones, *see* Jinny Jan
Midsummer Fair, *see* Widdecombe Fair
Oak and the Ash, The, *see* Rosemary Lane
Outlandish Knight, *see* Rich Nobleman
Seeds of Love, The, *see* Hostess's Daughter
Waukrife Minnie, *see* As I Walked Out
White Cockade, *see* Green Cockade

'Lor' bless y', the world be going that wicked the young chaps don't care for my songs. I reckon the end o' the world can't be over far off accordingly'

Foreword

It is a very changed world which sings these songs today. Sabine Baring-Gould (who lived from 1834–1924) often asked himself if the task of collecting the songs was worthwhile! Later he counted it the most important achievement of his life—in this he was certainly justified. Like Burns and Ramsay before him, Baring-Gould did much rewriting; some of it as in the case of 'Strawberry Fair' very justified at that time, for, had the original ballad been produced intact it would have fallen into disuse once again. Much of the rewriting, though, seems to have been done for its own sake. The words produced here have been taken directly from the 'fair copy' placed by Baring-Gould in Plymouth Public Library, and are produced here by kind permission of the city librarian, Mr W. Best Harris, and the trustees.

'Our folk music is a veritable moraine of rolled and ground fragments from musical strata far away. It contains songs of many centuries, all thrown together in a confused heap. What are the origins of these songs? It is impossible to say but some are ballads that have been handed down by the minstrels and troubadours of many continents; archaic melodies from before the Golden Age of Elizabeth' (Baring-Gould, essay from *English Minstrelsie*). There are songs influenced by the music hall of the day and by the spread of Methodism, and songs emanating from Vauxhall, Ranelagh and Marylebone Gardens. Many of the songs may have been composed or evolved by the singers themselves, 'for I do not think that the "rustic" was incapable of making poetry or music. To say that the ploughmen could not have originated melodies is mere assumption. Ploughmen have produced poetry, why not music? Burns was a ploughman, Clare was a farm lad, Bloomfield, a shoemaker and Tannahill, a weaver. The gifts were there' (Baring-Gould, 'Essay on Folk Song').

As well as the debt we owe to Baring-Gould for collecting these songs, our debt is still greater to all those singers who obstinately kept these songs alive. These old men, toothless, asthmatic, illiterate, were the sole source of such treasures. By far the greater number of songs was taken down from James Parsons, an illiterate hedger and thatcher whose father was an even greater singer called 'The Singing Machine'. It may well be that Parsons had descended from a family who were originally troubadours and who had settled on the land when the minstrels were put down by act of Parliament in 1597. He had a great predisposition towards archaic melodies and he was jealous that their character should not be changed. 'Now,' he would say (to Baring-Gould), 'I'll gie you a purty old tune as lively as they be made,' and he would strike up a song in one of the old church modes. He was an exacting master. 'Thicky wi'nt do,' he would say, 'You've gotten that note not right. You muṇ know that I'm the master and you'm the scholar; and I wi'nt have any slurs or blunders. What's right is right and what's wrong can never be right to the world's end.' At one time his master sent him to Lydford on the edge of Dartmoor to look after a farm he had bought. Whilst there, Parsons went every pay-day to a little moorland tavern, where the miners met to drink, and there he invariably got his 'entertainment' for his singing. 'I'd been zinging there,' said he, 'one evening till I got a bit fresh, and I thought 'twere time to be off. So I stood up to go and then one chap [Voysey] said to me, "Got to the end of your songs, old man?" "Not I," said I, "not by a long ways; but I reckon it be time for me to be going." "Looky here Jim," said Voysey, "I'll give you a quart of ale for every fresh song you sing us tonight." Well, I sat down again and I zinged on—I zinged sixteen fresh songs and Voysey had to pay for sixteen quarts . . . No zur, not pints, good English quarts. And then I hadn't come to the end o' my zongs, only I were that fuddled, I couldn't remember no more.'

Parsons met with a bad accident whilst cutting spears (ie pegs for thatching), on his knee; he had cut into a joint and the doctor feared he would never get over it. But he recovered, happily, to remember many more songs.

There was also Robert Hard an old stonebreaker, a cripple walking about on two sticks, from him songs were obtained only days before he died in a deep snowdrift; also James Olver, a tanner, a fine, hale old man with a skin fresh as a rose, silver hair and a grand patriarchal face. He came of a strict Methodist family and was only allowed to sing psalms and hymns at home. He nightly crept out of the house to hear the miners sing at an inn, these songs he remembered well. Then there was Jonas Coaker, the blind 'poet of the moor'. He was eighty-eight. 'I found him very feeble, lying in bed the greater part of the day but able to come down and sit by his peat fire for a couple of hours at noon. His voice was quite gone, he gave us the words and as we were not able to recover any of the melodies from him the captain of a neighbouring mine knew them and we noted them down from him' (Baring-Gould, 'Essay on Folk Song'). Singer Samuel Fone was deserted by his father when he was six. He recollects having made a waggon journey to London with his little sister. The journey took almost three days and they sang ballads the whole way. 'Sally Satterley was one of the very few women who gave us songs. She wouldn't stop still while she sang, because she would have forgotten the lines had she not been doing something. Consequently we had to follow her from the copper to the pigsty in order to obtain the songs.' She occupied a house that was built in a day because squatter's rights were obtained if the house was built and occupied in one day. Again, there were a score of others. James Masters of Broadstone, aged eighty-three; Edmund Fry, a thatcher; Matthew Baker, a poor old cripple of Lew Down, aged seventy-two; Helmore the miller, who died in Ivy Bridge Workhouse. We best remember them in their songs; they were certainly a happy breed.

Today, folk songs have come into their own again, our knowledge about them is greater than it was fifty years ago. With the advent of the guitar, styles of accompaniment have developed which are simple and most suitable for folk songs, although folk songs were, of course, invariably sung unaccompanied.

Neither the words nor the melodies are sacrosanct. The transmission of these orally will inevitably lead to changes. This is a natural process but the printed copy will remain for the coming generations.

There were many inaccuracies in the MS; verses which didn't fit melodies; both melodies and verses which were incomplete; lines that didn't scan properly. I have made the bare minimum of adjustment. Where the lines don't scan properly I have marked the beginning of bars or phrases, in some instances leaving the singer to make the adjustment himself. Where verses or lines were forgotten I have completed them and they are in brackets. Guitar chords have been supplied by Pat Shaw and these are sometimes different from the key in which the music is written.

G. H.

Folk Songs
of the
West Country

2. O once I could eat of the best,
    The best of good bread, only white,
   But am now glad, I trust, of a dry barley crust,
    And thankful to have it to bite.
    Refrain: Here's adieu, etc.

3. O once I could drink of the best,
    The best of ale humming and brown,
   But now I am glad if some water be had,
    That runneth from town unto town. *Refrain*

4. O once I was housed as the best,
    In mansion so well furnishèd,
   Now I'm thankful to catch my head under the thatch
    Of a pig-sty to shelter my head. *Refrain*

5. O once I was clothed in the best,
    Of broadcloth and linen fine spun,
   As naked as born to the dust I return,
    Thus neighbours my story is done. *Refrain*

A - hunting we will go

Taken down from J. Gerrard, an old man, nearly blind, at Cullyhole, near Chagford

1. Its of a jol-ly ploughing man, Was ploughing of his land, He cal-led to his hor-ses wo! And bid them patient stand. For a-
(It for)
hun-ting we will go, my boys, A - hun-ting we will go, A brave cock-ade all in my hat, We'll give the maids a show.

In C.

```
2/4 ⅞ |C - - - |G7 - - - |C - - - |(C7) - - - |

|G7 - - - |C - - - |G7 - - - |C - - - |
(or F - G7 - )           (F - G7 - )

|C - - - |F - G7 - |C - - - |Am - - - |
              (Am - Em - )

|F - - - |C - - - |G7 - - - |C - - ‖
```

Use Capo at the 2nd fret for Key D.

    2. He sat himself all on his plough,
       To sing he did begin,
     His voice was so melodious, too,
       It made the horse bells ring.
      Refrain: For [a-nutting] we will go my boys, etc.

3. A pretty maid came tripping by
    With basket on her arm,
   She thought to hear the ploughman sing,
    It for certain was no harm.   *Refrain*

4. He took her to a shady grove,
    His courage for to show,
   He put his arms about her waist,
    And laid the fair maid low.   *Refrain*

5. And when he'd had his will of her,
    He raised her from the ground,
   She said, with the ploughing man,
    I see the world go round.   *Refrain*

6. He went unto his horses then,
    To end his pleasant song,
   He said: 'My sweet and pretty maid,
    Your mother'll think you long.'   *Refrain*

7. Come all you pretty maidens fair,
    Take warning by my rhyme,
   And if you do a-nutting go,
    I pray be home in time.   *Refrain*

8. For if that you should stay too long,
    To hear the ploughman sing,
   Perhaps a young farmer you may have,
    To nurse all in the spring.   *Refrain*

Also taken down from Robert Hard at Menheniot and James Parsons. Baring-Gould felt constrained to tone down the words but I have given the original as in the MS. E. J. Moeran collected a version from Suffolk, see 'Nutting Song', in Six Suffolk Folk Songs. *The refrain runs 'A-nutting we will go' and this is probably correct.*

As I walked out

(I'm seventeen come Sunday)

Taken down from Edmund Fry, Lydford, in 1889

2. O ' where are you going my fair pretty maid?
   O where are you going my lambie?
   Then ' cheerfully she answered me,
   An errand for my mammie.
   Refrain: With a fa la la, fa la la la la,
   An errand for my mammie.

3. How ' old are you my fair pretty maid?
   How old are you my honey?
   Then ' cheerfully she answered me,
   I'm seventeen come Sunday. *Refrain*

4. Will you ' take a man, my fair pretty maid,
   Will you take a man my lambie?
   Then ' cheerfully she answered me,
   I dare not for my mammie. *Refrain*

5. If ' you will come to my mother's house,
   When the moon is shining clearly,
   I'll ' lift the pin and let you in,
   And my mammie will not hear me. *Refrain*

6. O ' then I went to her mother's house,
   When the moon was brightly shining,
   Then she ' lifted the pin and let me in,
   And we lay with our arms entwining. *Refrain*

7. Then she ' said to me, Will you marry me?
   As she let me out in the morning,
   For by ' thee I'm one as is quite undone,
   O leave me not in scorning. *Refrain*

8. Then she ' said to me, Will you marry me?
   O say this now or never,
   For if ' that you are not good and true,
   Then I am undone forever. *Refrain*

This is better known as 'I'm Seventeen Come Sunday', as collected by Cecil Sharp and Kidson. The version in Canow Kernow (1966) *says, 'The melody and first verse were found at St Ives Museum in a MS marked "Cornish Folk Songs".' The original ballad was altered by Burns to 'The Waukrife Minnie' for Johnson's* Musical Museum. *The words are on broadsides by Such and by Bebbington, Manchester.*

Banks of Sweet Primeroses

Taken down from J. Woodrich and W. Nicholls

1. One mid-sum-mer morning as I was a-walk-ing, To view the fields and take the air, 'Twas down by the banks of sweet prim-è-ros-es, That I beheld a maiden fair.

In D.

6/8 ≁	D - - A7 - -	D - - Bm - -
F♯m - - Bm - -	E7 - - A7 - -	Bm(orD)- - Bm - -
Em - - Bm - - |F♯m - - Bm - - |Em - A7 D -	

For Key E use Capo at the 2nd fret and play as for D.

2. With ' three long steps I ' came up to her,
   Not ' knowing her as ' she passed by,
   I ' stepped up to her, I was ' thinking to woo her
   And ' ask the reason that ' she did cry.

3. Oh ' where are you going to my ' pretty maiden,
   Oh ' where are you going on ' this lonely way,
   I'll ' make you as happy as ' any fine lady,
   If ' you will but answer me ' with a yea.

4. Stand ' off, stand off, you ' gay deceiver,
   You ' are most false of ' all false men,
   It's ' you that have caused all my ' ache and sorrow,
   To ' give me comfort ' is in vain.

5. I'll ′ go and seek some ′ lonesome valley,
    Where ′ none on earth my ′ face shall see,
  Where ′ small pretty birds do ′ change their voices,
    And ′ refuge seek from ′ love and thee.

6. You ′ pretty maids that ′ go a-courting,
    ′ Pray give heed to ′ what I say,
  There's ′ many a bright sun′shiny morning,
    That ′ turneth to a ′ rainy day.

I had the greatest difficulty in fitting the words to the melody, and as singers were very indifferent to the number of syllables in one line I have been constrained to omit some words to make the verses scan properly. 'Banks of Sweet Primeroses' in midsummer? Never mind, it sings well! It is noted that the tune and words show a remarkable constancy through several versions collected.

Bonny Blue Handkerchief

Taken down from John Woodrich, locally known as "Ginger Jack"

1. One morn-ing so ear-ly I chanced for to stray, A sweet pret-ty maiden came trip-ping my way, With cheeks as red ro-ses she blithe-ly did sing, With a bon-ny blue handkerchief tied un-der her chin.

In C.

```
3/4 ⁊ |C - F |C - - |C - G7 |C - - |
|C - - |G - D7 |G - D7 |G - - |
|C - - |F - - |C - - |G7 - - |
|C - F |C - - |G7 - - |C -  ||
```

2. Where so ' fast maid, I ' said, and ' caught her by the ' waist,
   I'm ' going to my ' mother, she ' said, I'm in ' haste,
   To ' work I be ' going, to ' sit and to ' spin,
   With my ' bonny blue ' handkerchief tied ' under my ' chin.

3. Then why ' wear you that ' kerchief ' tied round your ' head?
   Tis the ' country ' fashion, kind ' sir, then she ' said,
   And the ' fashion, you ' see, sir, I ' like to be ' in,
   With my ' bonny blue ' handkerchief tied ' under my ' chin.

4. To ' kiss her sweet ' lips then I ' sought to be'gin,
   O ' stay, sir, she ' said, ere a ' kiss you would ' win,
   Pray ' let me first ' see, sir, a ' gold wedding ' ring,
   O the ' bonny blue ' handkerchief tied ' under my ' chin.

5. Why ' wear you that ' kerchief, sweet ' maiden, I ' said,
   Be ' cause, sir, the ' colour is ' not one to ' fade,
   As a ' sailor's blue ' jacket who ' fights for the ' King.
   So's my ' bonny blue ' handkerchief tied ' under my ' chin.

6. With ' gold and with ' silver I ' tried all in ' vain,
   She ' smiled in my ' face, with a ' scornful dis'dain,
   Crying, ' sir, tis not ' gold can a ' kiss from me ' earn,
   From my ' bonny blue ' handkerchief tied ' under my ' chin.

7. For this ' bonny blue ' handkerchief my ' love gave to ' me,
   He ' told me the ' colour was ' ne'er false, do you ' see?
   And to ' him I'll prove ' true as the ' colour that's ' in,
   In this ' bonny blue ' handerkchief tied ' under my ' chin.

8. When he ' heard her so ' loyal, he ' could not for'bear,
   He ' flew to her ' arms and he ' called her his ' dear,
   Saying, my ' dearest ' jewel, here ' *is* the gold ' ring,
   To that ' bonny blue ' handkerchief tied ' under the ' chin.

9. To ' Church then they ' went and were ' married with ' speed,
   And ' this loving ' couple lived ' happy in'deed,
   When their ' day's work is ' over, they ' cheerfully ' sing,
   'O the ' bonny blue ' handkerchief tied ' under the chin.'

The first verse not recollected by Woodrich but taken from broadsides. The words have appeared with slight variations on broadsides by Catnach, etc. There is a companion to it, 'The Bonny Blue Jacket', on broadsides.

The Carpenter's Wife

Taken down from J. Paddon, Holcombe Burnell. 1889

Alternative in E minor:-

```
6/8 𝄾  |Em - - Am - - |B7 - - Em - - |C - - G - - |

    |D7 - - G - - |C - - D - - |Em - C B7 - - |

    |Em - - B7 - - |C7 - B7 Em - ||
```

2. O my ' husband he is a carpenter,
    A ' carpenter ' good is he.
    By ' him I have gotten a little son
    Or ' else I would go, sweet ' love, with thee.

3. But if ' I should leave my husband dear,
    My ' fair sweet ' boy also,
    O ' what have you got far far away
    That ' along with thee I should ' go?

4. I have ' seven ships that sail on the sea,
    ' It was one brought ' me to land.
    I have ' mariners many to wait on thee
    To ' be, sweet love, at ' thy command.

5. She ' had not been long upon the sea,
    Not ' long upon the deep,
    Be'fore that she was wringing her hands
    And ' loudly did wail and ' weep.

6. O ' why do you wail and wherefore weep
    And ' wring your hands? said he.
    Do you ' weep for the gold that lies in the hold
    Or ' do you weep for my ' fee?

7. I ' do not weep for your gold, she said,
    ' Nor yet do I weep for your fee,
    But by the ' mast-head is my baby dead
    And I ' weep for my dead ba'by.

8. She ' had not a-been upon the seas
    But ' six days of the week
    Be'fore that she lay as cold as the clay
    And ' never a word could ' speak.

9. They ' had not a sailed upon the seas
    Of ' weeks but three and four
    But ' down to the bottom the ship did swim
    And ' never was heard of ' more.

10. And ' when the news to England came
    The ' carpenter's wife was drowned
    The ' carpenter rent his hair and wept
    And ' then as dead he ' swound.

The full twenty verses of this ballad may be seen in The Everlasting Circle.

Chase the Buffalo

Taken down from J. Benoy, at Menheniot

2. Come ' all you pretty maidens, and spin us up some yarn,
   To ' make us some clothing to keep us snug and warm,
   You can ' card and you can spin, maids, and we can reap and mow.
   Refrain: And we'll ' lie down, etc.

3. There are ' fishes in the sea, that are fitting for our use,
   And ' high and lofty sugar canes to yield us pleasant juice,
   There is ' all sorts of game, boys, beside the buck and doe. *Refrain*

4. Sup'pose the wild Indians by chance should come too near,
   We would ' link us heart to heart, and have nothing to fear,
   We would ' march through the town, boys and give the fatal blow. *Refrain*

Sung also by James Olver and J. Parsons to the same air. A similar text is given in W. A. Barrett's English Folk Songs, *with a note that 'this is an emigrant's song, and probably belongs to the early part of the eighteenth century'.*

Coasts of Barbary

Taken down from an old tramp in North Devon

Use Capo

2. There is ' nothing ahead, sir, there is nothing astern,
   But a ' lofty ship to windward doth on us turn.

3. Then ' hail her, hail her! our noble captain cried,
   Are ' you a man of war or a pirateer, he cried.

4. I ' am no man of war, no pirateer today,
   But a ' saucy pirate I, that seeketh for my prey.

5. Then ' broadside to broadside, these gallant vessels go,
   Away ' the English the (saucy) pirates mast did blow.

6. For ' mercy! for mercy! the daring rascals cried,
   But the ' mercy we showed them was to sink them in the tide.

7. With ' cutlass or gun, they fought for hours three,
    The ' ship it was their coffin, their grave it was the sea.

The song appears in Cecil Sharp's Folk Songs from Somerset *and Ashton's* Real Sailors' Songs. *It is in some respects much like 'The Golden Vanity'.*

2. Remember Job a patient man,
   All wealthy in the East,
   He was reduced to poverty.
   His sorrows sure increased.
   But he bore all might honestly,
   And did from wrath refrain,
   And, as he trusted in the Lord,
   He soon grew rich again.

3. Tho' poor I be, I'm well content,
   For riches do not crave,
   For earthly wealth or vanity,
   On this side of the grave.
   Tho' many swell in riches great,
   They think their luck to flout,
   We nothing brought into the world,
   And nothing carry out.

4. Come all ye worthy Christian men,
   That wander through the towns,
   That ask a lodging where to lie,
   That often sleep on downs.
   The time will very shortly come,
   When wandering will be o'er,
   The gates of pearl will then unfurl,
   And we shall rove no more.

5. Come all ye worthy Christian men,
   That hunger and are poor,
   Remember greedy Lazarus,
   Lay at the rich man's door.
   A-begging for the crumbs of bread,
   That from his table fell,
   A little while and all is changed,
   He now in heaven does dwell.

6. The time is coming on so fast,
   When parted men must be,
   The only distance that remains,
   Is joy and misery.
   And we must give a strict account,
   The big as well as small,
   Then recollect ye Christian men,
   One God will judge us all.

2. Solomon in all his glory,
   Told us quite another story,
   In our cups to sing and glory,
   When we're met together.
   Come let's live and we'll agree,
   Always shun bad company,
   Why should we not merry (merry) be,
   When we're met together.
   Refrain: Solomon, etc.

3. Keep from quarrelling and fighting,
   Evil speaking and back-biting,
   All these things take no delight in,
   When we're met together.
   Come let's live, etc. . . .
   Refrain: Keep from, etc.

Olver acquired the song at Liskeard in 1828, from G. Brooks of Grampound. Olver knew only one verse, the rest from Fry, and completed by me.   G.H.

Constant Johnny

Taken down from Roger Luxton, Halwell, 1889

1. Con-stant John-ny— I— do— love thee, There's none o - ther—

I— do a-dore, 'Tis your de-ceit-ful heart, Causes me to feel this smart,

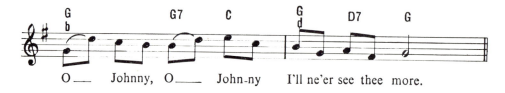
O— Johnny, O— John-ny I'll ne'er see thee more.

2. HE: Charming Molly, I do love thee,
   There's none other I do adore,
     See what your eyes have done,
       'Tis that I feel this wound,
   No Molly, No Molly, I'll not see thee more.

3. SHE: When she saw young Johnny bleeding,
   Down at Cupids fairy bower,
     'Tis your deceitful heart,
       Causes me to feel this smart,
   O Johnny, O Johnny, I am thine this hour.

4. BOTH: Now this couple they got married,
   And in wedlock's chains are sure,
     They now together dwell,
       None can them excel;
   O Johnny, O Molly, we shall part no more.

The song is a dialogue and such dialogues were commonly sung in farmhouses. The air has a certain Vauxhall Gardens sophistication about it.

Cuckoo

Taken down from Robert Hard, 1892 and Mary Langworthy at Stoke Fleming, 1892.

Use Capo at the 2nd fret for Key D.

2. O ' meeting is a pleasure but parting is grief,
   An ' inconstant lover is worse than a thief.
   A ' thief can but rob me of all that I have
   But an ' inconstant lover will send me to the grave.

3. The ' grave will receive me and bring me to dust,
   An ' inconstant lover no maiden can trust.
   They'll ' court you and kiss you, poor maids to deceive,
   There's ' not one in twenty that one may believe.

4. Come ' all you fair maidens wherever you be,
   Don't ' hang your poor hearts on the sycamore tree.
   The ' leaf it will wither, the roots will decay
   And ' if I'm forsaken I perish away.

This charming little song was known throughout England. It is to be found in an old Garland The Sailor's Return *(Glasgow, 1802),* Halliwell's Nursery Rhymes *and Dr Barnett's* English Folk Songs. *The significance of this song seems to be this: the inconstant lover is likened first to a cuckoo that is a rover and lastly to a sycamore tree that drops its leaves so early.*

Emigrant's Song

Taken down from Mary Treese aged 88, Menheniot, by F. W. B. April 1891.
On broadsides by Such (No. 142) and Catnach

1. I'm a strang-er in this coun-try From A-mer-i-ca I come, I'm a strang-er in this coun-try I'll tar-ry here a-while And then I'll ram-ble fur-ther For many a long mile.

There's no one here does know me, They do not know my name.

In C.
3/4 ⁊ |C - F |C - - |G7 - - |
C - :		-	Am - -	Em - -
Am - D7	G - G7	C - F
Em(or C) - Am	Dm7 - G7	C -	

Use Capo

2. Some ' say that I am rakish,
    And ' some do call me wild,
Some ' say that I am rakish,
    And ' many maids beguiled,
But to ' prove that I am loyal,
    Come ' on, sweet love, with me,
I'll ' take you to America,
    My ' darling you shall be.

3. O ' give my love to Polly,
    The ' maiden I adore,
And ' give my love to Sally,
    Al'though she is so poor,
And ' give my love to Betty,
    My ' love and my delight,
My ' love likewise to Hetty,
    I ' dream of her at night.

4. The ' moon shall set in darkness,
    The ' stars shall give no light,
If ' ever I deceitful prove,
    To ' my dear heart's delight,
All ' in the midst of ocean,
    Shall ' spring the myrtle tree,
If ' ever I unfaithful prove,
    To ' her that goes with me.

Evening Prayer

At one time this was the only Prayer used by the village children and was cut down to one verse. The complete song was obtained from a woman in the workhouse at Tavistock.

1. Matthew, Mark, and Luke and John,
Bless the bed that I lie on,
Four angels to my bed,
Two to pillow, two to head,
Two to hear me when I pray,
Two to bear my soul away.

The bracketed note at the end is in the original, but this seems to be a corruption as may be seen by comparing the previous terminations. The melody is thus in the Phrygian Mode

*Use Capo at the 3rd fret for Eb

2. Monday morn the week begin,
      Christ deliver our souls from sin.
   Tuesday morn nor curse, nor swear,
      Christes Body that will tear.
   Wednesday, middle of the week,
      Woe to the soul Christ does not seek.

3. Thursday morn, Saint Peter wrote,
      Joy to the soul that heaven hath bote.*
   Friday Christ died on the tree
      To save other men as well as me.
   Saturday, sure, the evening dead,
      Sunday morn, the Book's outspread.

4. God is the branch and I the flower,
      Pray God send me a blessed hour.
   I go to bed, some sleep to take,
      The Lord, He knows if I shall wake.
   Sleep I ever, sleep I never,
      God receive my soul for ever.

   *Bote—bid for

Flora, Lily of the West

Taken down from Henry Hawken, 1899, also from Matthew Baker and Samuel Fone

2. Her ' golden hair in ringlets hung, her dress was spangled o'er,
   With rings on every finger, brought from a foreign shore,
   'Twould en'tice kings and princes, so costly was she dressed,
   And she excels fair Venus—she's the Lily of the West.

3. I ' courted her awhile and in hopes her love to gain,
   But soon she turned her back on me, which caused me grievous pain,
   She robbed me of my liberty, she stole from me my rest,
   I roam, forsook by Flora, the Lily of the West.

4. One ' day as I was walking, down in a shady grove,
   I spied a lord of high degree conversing with my love,
   She sang a song melodiously, whilst I was sore oppressed
   And said adieu to Flora, the Lily of the West.

5. I ' walked up to my rival with a dagger in my hand,
   I seized him from my false love and bid him boldly stand,
   Then mad with desperation, I swore I'd pierce his breast,
   For I was betrayed by Flora, the Lily of the West.

6. Then ' I did stand my trial and boldly made my plea,
   A flaw was in the indictment, which quickly set me free,
   That beauty bright I did adore, the judge did he molest,
   Saying, Go you faithless Flora, the Lily of the West.

7. So its ' now I've gained my liberty, a wooing I will go,
   I'll ramble through old Ireland, I'll travel Scotland through,
   Although she wore my life away, she still disturbs my rest,
   I must ramble for my Flora, the Lily of the West.

The song was sung at the Revel Inn in St Breward by an old man in 1899. Published in Songs of the West *no 58, where the trial was cut out. I have reinstated verses 4, 5, 6 and 7. Baring-Gould says that the ballad is Irish (note verse 7) and that the air is characteristic of Irish melodies. It is known in America and is sung by Joan Baez. It was also collected by Helen Creighton in Nova Scotia, where the scene is set in America. The words are on broadsheets by Such, Fortey and Barr.*

The Foolish Boy

Words from Daniel Radford, Mount Tavy, Tavistock, who heard the tune and words forty years ago sung by an old ploughman. 1888

2. I sold my six horses and bought me a cow,
   I'm a going to get money but I can't tell how.

3. I sold my cow and I bought me a calf.
   By that my bargain I lost just half.

4. I sold my calf and bought me a cat
   And in the chimney corner the pretty creature sat.

5. I sold my cat and I bought me a mouse
   Set fire to her tail and her burnt down the house.

6. I sold my mouse and I bought me a wife.
   Her cut my throat with an old rusty knife.

The Forsaken Maiden

Taken down from Jas. Parsons, 1888

1. A maiden sat a weeping Down by the sea-shore. What ails my pretty Sally? What ails my pretty Sally, And makes her heart sore.

In A minor

Use Capo

2. Because I am a-weary
    A-weary in my mind.
   No comfort and no pleasure,
    No comfort and no pleasure
   Henceforth can I find.

3. I'll spread my sail of silver,
    I'll loose my rope of silk.
   My mast is of the cypress tree,
    My mast is of the cypress tree,
   My track is white as milk.

4. I'll spread my sail of silver,
       I'll steer toward the sun,
   And thou, false love, will weep for me,
       And thou, false love, will weep for me,
   For me when I'm gone.

Also taken down from Will Huggett, Chagford: both are identical. Baring-Gould says the tune is probably of the sixteenth century.

The Golden Vanity

Taken down from Jas. Olver, Launceston, 1889

2. To the captain then upspake the little cabin-boy,
   He said, What is my fee, if the galley I destroy?
   The Spanish Ga-la-lie, if no more it shall annoy,
   As you sail by the low-lands low.

3. Of silver and gold I will give to you a store;
    And my pretty little daughter that dwelleth on the shore,
Of treasure and of fee as well, I'll give to thee galore,
    As we sail by the low-lands low.

4. Then the boy bared his breast, and straightway leaped in,
    And he held all in his hand, an augur sharp and thin,
And he swam until he came to the Spanish galleon,
    As she lay by the low-lands low.

5. He bore'd with the augur, he bored once and twice,
    And some were playing cards, and some were playing dice,
When the water flowed in it dazzled their eyes,
    And she sank by the low-lands low.

6. So the cabin-boy did swim all to the larboard side,
    Saying captain! take me in, I am drifting with the tide!
I will shoot you! I will kill you! the cruel captain cried,
    You may sink by the low-lands low.

7. Then the cabin-boy did swim all to the starboard side
    Saying, Messmates take me in, I am drifting with the tide!
Then they laid him on the deck, and he closed his eyes and died,
    As they sailed by the low-lands low.

8. They sewed his body up, all in an old cow's hide,
    And they cast the gallant cabin-boy, over the ship's side,
And left him without more ado a-drifting with the tide,
    And to sink by the low-lands low.

Green Besoms

Taken down from Will Huggins, Mason, Lydford, 1888

```
In E                                    C#m  -   -   -
2/4  {   |E  -  A  -  |B  -  B7  -  |(or E  -  B7   -  |
                           a             g#        f#
 B7       E7
|E   -    E7  - ) |A  -  E  -  |F#m -  A  -  |B  -  F#7  -  |
                        g#
|B  -  B7  -  |E (or G#m) - -  |E  -  -  -  |C#m -  -  -  |
              a    g#
|F#m -  B  -  |G#m  -  -  -  |C#m  -  -  -  |F#  -  B7  -  |
|E  -  -  ||B7  |E  -  A  -  |B  -  -  -  |C#m -  F#7 -  |
|.              |/      g#
|B7  -  -  -  |C#m  -  -  -  |B7(or G#m  -  E7  -  |
|A  -  E  -  |F#m -  B7  -  |E  -  B7  -  |E  -       ||
        g#
```

2. One day as I was trudging
   Down by my native cot
   I saw a jolly farmer,
   O happy is his lot.
   He ploughs his furrows deep,
   The seed he layeth low,
   And there it bides asleep
   Until the green broom blow.

3. One day as I was walking
   'Twas down in yonder vale
   I met Jack Spratt the miller
   That taketh toll and tale.
   His mill, O how it rattles,
   The grist it grindeth clean.
   I ease him of his jingling
   By selling besoms green.

4. One day as I was walking
   Across the hills so high
   I saw the wealthy squire
   Who hath a rolling eye.
   I sing my song, he tips a wink,
   And glad the squire did seem.
   I ease him of his jingling chink
   By selling besoms green.

5. One day as I was walking
   Along the King's high-way
   I met the parson riding
   And ventured him to stay.
   The parish tithe that is your due
   Collecting you have been,
   But tithe I'll also take of you
   By selling besoms green.

6. O when the yellow broom is ripe
   Upon its native soil
   It's like a pretty baby bright
   With sweet and wavily smile.
   My cuts that make the besom
   I bundle tight and spare
   All honest folks to please 'em
   I'm the darling of the fair.

The Green Cockade

Taken down from Edmund Fry

2. Leave off your grief and sorrow,
　　And quit this doleful strain,
　I'll think of you so truly
　　Whilst marching o'er the plain
　When I return we'll marry,
　　By this cockade I swear,
　Your heart must not be breaking,
　　For the love to me you bear.

3. O may you never prosper
　　O may you never thrive!
　Nor anything you take in hand,
　　As long as you're alive.
　The very ground you tread upon
　　The grass refuse to grow,
　Since you have brought upon my heart
　　Such sorrow grief and woe.

4. But since he's gone and left me
　　In sorrow for to mourn,
　I wish the wars were over
　　And my love is safe returned.
　But since he's gone and left me
　　I am resolved to rove,
　And carve his name on every tree,
　　That grows in yonder grove.

Baring-Gould says, 'As we heard the song, the cockade was described as green, but there never was a green cockade. A Barnstaple punch-bowl with cover, at Altarnun in Cornwall, has on the cover a figure of a piper with his dog and the inscription: "Piper, play us the White Cockade."' It was published in Songs of the West *as 'The White Cockade'. In* Canow Kernow (1966), *this is refuted. Miss J. Kelynack wrote that she had found in a book called* The Foster Brothers of Doon *the statement that 'In the Irish Rebellion of 1798 the rebels wore a green cockade. A green cockade was also worn by William III's army when it invaded Ireland.'* Canow Kernow *gives a slightly different version from our own. The last verse from 'The Duke of Gordon's Garland.' Edmund Fry couldn't remember verse three.*

Greenland Whale Fishery

Taken down from R. Gregory, Twobridges, 1890

2. In ' eighteen hundred and twenty-four
     On ' March the twenty-third
   We ' hoist our colours to the mast head
     And for ' Greenland bore away, brave boys,
   And for ' Greenland bore away.

3. John ' Paigent was our captain's name,
     Our ' ship the Lion bold.
   We weighèd anchor at the bow
     To ' face the storm and cold, brave boys,
   And to ' Greenland bore away.

4. We ' were twelve gallant men on board
     And ' to the north did steer,
   Old ' England left we in our wake,
     We ' sailors know not fear, brave boys,
   And to ' Greenland bore away.

5. Our ' boatswain to the mast head went
     With a ' spy-glass in his hand.
   He ' cries, A Whale! a whale-fish blows,
     She ' blows at every span, brave boys,
   And to ' Greenland bear away.

6. Our ' captain on the quarter-deck
     A ' violent man was he,
   He ' swore the devil should take us all
     If that ' fish were lost to we, brave boys,
   And to ' Greenland bear away.

7. Our ' captain on the quarter-deck
     A ' violent man was he,
   O'er'haul! o'erhaul! he loudly cried,
     And ' launch our boat to sea, brave boys,
   And to ' Greenland bear away.

8. Our ′ boat being launched and all hands in
    The ′ whale was full in view,
Re′solved was every sea-man bold
    To ′ steer where the whale-fish blew, brave boys,
And to ′ Greenland bear away.

9. The ′ whale was struck, the line paid out,
    She ′ gave a flash with the tail.
The ′ boat capsized, we lost five men
    And ′ never caught the whale, brave boys,
And to ′ Greenland bear away.

10. Bad ′ news we to the captain brought,
    We'd ′ lost five prentice boys,
Then ′ down his colours he did haul
    At ′ hearing the sad news, brave boys,
And from ′ Greenland bore away.

11. The ′ losing of the whale, said he,
    Doth ′ grieve my heart full sore,
But the ′ losing of my five brave men
    Doth ′ grieve me ten times more, brave boys,
And from ′ Greenland bore away.

12. The ′ winter star doth now appear
    So, ′ boys, the anchor weigh,
'Tis ′ time to leave the cold country
    And for ′ England bear away, brave boys,
And from ′ Greenland bear away.

This is a very old song and exists in several variants. It has been adapted to several captains, with their unsuccessful fishings. Stanza 2 gives no real clue to the date of the song. It appears as a black-letter ballad in a Collection of Old Ballads *(1725). Our 'Greenland Fishery' appears on a broadside by Catnach and is reprinted among Such broadsides. A version is given by Cecil Sharp in* Folk Songs from Somerset.

Henry Martyn

Taken down from Roger Luxton, Hallwell, 1889

1. In merry Scotland, in merry Scotland, There lived brothers three, brothers three, — They all did cast lots which of them should go, should go, should go, — A robbing upon the salt sea.

Use Capo at fifth fret.

2. The lot it fell upon Henry Martyn,
   The youngest of the three,
   That he should go rob on the salt, salt sea,
   To maintain his brothers and he.

3. He had not a sailed a long winter's night,
    Nor yet a short winter's day,
  Before he espied a gay merchant ship,
    Come sailing along that way.

4. How far, how far, cried Henry Martyn,
    How far are you going? said he
  For I am a robber upon the salt seas,
    To maintain my brothers and me.

5. Stand off, stand off! the captain he cried,
    The lifeguards they are aboard.
  My cannons are loaden with powder and shot;
    And every man hath a sword.

6. For three long hours they merrily fought,
    For hours they fought full three.
  And many a blow it dealt many a wound,
    As they fought on the salt, salt sea.

7. 'Twas broadside against a broadside then,
    And at it, the which should win,
  A shot in the gallant ship bored a hole,
    And then did the water rush in.

8. Bad news! bad news, for old England
    Bad news has come to the town,
  The king his vessel is wrecked and lost,
    And all his brave soldiers drown.

9. Bad news! bad news through the London street!
    Bad news has come to the king,
  The lives of his guard they be all a lost,
    O the tidings be sad that I bring.

See Child 167, and Traditional Tunes of the Child Ballads, Bronson p.133

Her contented farmer's Son
Taken down from J. Woodrich, labourer, Broadwood, 1892

1. 'Tis of a merchant's daughter, In London Town did dwell, So modest and so handsome, her parents loved her well. They did admire both Lord and Squire But all their suits were vain, For there was none save a farmer's son, That maidens heart could gain, that maidens heart could gain.

v. 5 Her contented farmer's son, Her contented farmer's son,

In E
```
4
4  ?     |E -  B7 -  |E -  -  E  |E -  B7 -  |
|E -  -  -  |E -  B7 -  |E -  -  -  |B -  B7 -  |
|E -  -  -  |E -  -  -  |E -  -  -  |A -  -  -  |
|B -  -  B7  |E -  B7 -  |E -  -  -  |
|E -  A -  |E -  B  B7  |C#m - F#m B7  |E -  -  ||
```
Use Capo

2. Long time young William courted her,
    And fixed the wedding day,
  Her parents both were nothing loth,
    Her brothers they said Nay.
  But there was a lord who had pledged his word,
    That him she should not shun,
  We will waylay and then will slay
    The contented farmer's son.

3. A fair was held not far from town
    The brothers went straight away,
  And asked young William's company,
    With them to pass the day.
  But mark, returning home again,
    They swore his race was won,
  And with a stake his life did take;
    Of the contented farmer's son.

4. These villians then returned home,
    And sister, they did say,
  From thought remove thy inconstant love,
    And put him clean away.
  The truth we tell, in love he fell,
    With some fair other one,
  Therefore we came to tell the same,
    Of the contented farmer's son.

5. As on her pillow Mary lay,
    She dreamt a dreadful dream,
  She thought she saw his body lie,
    As floating in a stream,
  Then she arose, drew on her clothes,
    And to seek her love did run,
  When dead and cold she did behold,
    He contented farmer's son.

6. The salten tears upon her cheek,
    Were mingled in his gore,
  She tried in vain to ease her pain,
    And kissed him ten times o'er.
  She gathered leaves and ashen heaps
    To keep him from the sun,
  One night and day thus passed away,
    With her contented farmer's son.

7. But hunger it came creeping on,
    The maiden shook with woe,
  To try to find his murderer,
    She straight way home did go,
  Says, parents dear, pray list and hear,
    A dreadful deed is done,
  In yonder vale, he's dead and pale,
    My contented farmer's son.

8. Her eldest brother then outspake,
    I slew him not, said he;
  The same replied the younger one,
    And swore most solemnly.
  But Mary said: why turn so red?
    You seek the law to shun,
  You've done the deed and you shall bleed,
    For my contented farmer's son.

9. The brothers soon their guilt did own,
    And for the same did die,
  But Mary fair, in deep despair,
    She never ceased to cry.
  The parents they did fade away,
    Their glass of life outrun,
  The maiden bride, in sorrow died,
    For her contented farmer's son.

The original ballad is found on broadsides by Ross of Newcastle, Such and others. Baring-Gould gives it in *Songs of the West* at no 69, but wrote entirely new words for it. Versions are given in *Folk Song Journal, vol 1, p 160*.

Highwayman

Taken down from J. Townsend, Holne, 1890

1. I went to London both blithe and gay,
   My time I wasted in bowls and play,
   Until my cash it did get low,
   And then on the highway I was forced to go.

Alternative and possibly better harmonization ✳ — ✳

```
|G  -  -    |D7 G  G  |C  Am C  |D7    G || 
 b           a  g           b
```

*In C

```
3/4 ↆ |C  -  -   |F  -  Am |Dm  -  -  |
    |G7 -  -   |Em -  -  |Dm  Am -  |
    |Dm (or F) -  -   |G7    C     ||
```
*Use Capo

2. O ' next I took me a pretty wife,
   I ' loved her dear as I loved my life,
   But for ' to maintain her both fine and gay
   Re'solved I was that the world should pay.

3. I ' robbed Lord Edgcumbe I do declare
   And ' Lady Templar of Melbourne Square.
   I ' bade them good night, sat ' in my chair,
   With ' laughter and song went to my dear.

4. I ′ robbed them of five hundred pounds so bright
    But ′ all of it squandered one jovial night,
    Till ′ taken by such as I never knew,
    But I ′ was informed they were Fielding's crew.

5. The ′ judge his mercy he did extend,
    He ′ pardoned my crime, bade me amend,
    But ′ still I pursued a thriving trade.
    I ′ always was reckoned a roving blade.

6. O ′ now I'm judged and doomed to die
    And ′ many a maid for me will cry,
    For ′ all their sighs and for all salt tear
    Where ′ I shall go the Lord knows where.

7. My ′ father he sighs and he makes his moan,
    My ′ mother she weeps for her darling son,
    But ′ sighs and tears will never save
    Nor ′ keep me from an untimely grave.

According to Margaret Dean-Smith's A Guide to English Folk Song Collections, *this might be called the archetype of the execution ballad. The gist of the condemned man's apology is an early marriage to a wife of expensive tastes, highway robbery to maintain her in luxury and a descent thence to burglary, capture and execution. The ballad enjoyed a vogue over a long period.*

Hostess's Daughter

Taken down from Jas. Masters, Broadstone, 1891

1. To London Town when first I came, Then no one knew my face or name, And there four months I did remain, I stayed at Smithfield at an Inn, The hostess had a daughter fair, With waving locks of coalblack hair, And eyes as coals that glowing were, They were so bright so glistening.

2. I kissed her rosy cheeks and brow,
   Her face was mingled blood and snow,
   We loved each other well I know,
      We loved each other tenderly.
   I sowed the silly seeds of love,
   I sowed them in a garden grove,
   And now I must away remove,
      From London Town away must fly.

3. The seeds of love they grew apace,
   The tears were ever on her face,
   I would not tarry in that place,
      To reap the harvest I had sown.
   Now when the pretty babe is born,
   Twill lie within her bosom warm,
   But ne'er be danced upon the arms,
      Of father, for that babe has none.

Baring-Gould included it in Songs of the West *at no 70 and states that 'the coarseness of the original words obliged me to rewrite the song'. The song was also taken down from James Parsons but some of the song was 'too gross' and apparently not noted. This song has become intermingled with 'The Seeds of Love' which may be of earlier origin.*

In Bibberly Town

Taken down from J. Bennett, labourer, Chagford, 1890

1. In Bib-ber-ly Town a maid did dwell, O! a bux-om lass I knew right well, Her age it was but twen-ty two And O! for a man she had in view. Re fol-di-ral-li-ro, Re fal-di-ral-doo, And O! for a man she had in view.

    2. This maid being generous, kind and free,
        Went to dwell with a squire of high degree,
      The tinker he came to try his metal,
      And he asked if he should mend the kettle.
      Refrain: Re fol, etc . . . (dettle)

    3. The maiden said we shall soon agree,
        The table is spread come dine with me,
      He ate and he drank, and 'Here,' he said,
        'I drink to the health of a fine, pretty maid!'
      Refrain: Re fol, etc . . . (day)

    4. Then he up with his arm about her waist,
        'The best of dishes I have yet to taste!'
      He took her, he whisked her behind the door,
      And there he kissed times a score.
      Refrain: Re fol, etc . . . (daw)

5. And when he had kissed her five times four,
    O then he slipped from behind the door,
'O prithee sweet tinker receive thy fee',
    And she put in his hand full five guinea.
    Refrain: Re fol, etc . . . (dee)

6. He went to the ale house standing by,
    And he said: 'O rich as a Lord am I,
'I'll sit and I'll drink of your best,' quoth he,
    'Until I have spent my five guinea.'
    Refrain: Re fol, etc . . . (dee)

7. 'And when it is spent away I'll fare,
    For kettles to mend all everywhere,
Five guineas in gold are mine and more
    When I kiss a maiden behind the door.'
    Refrain: Re fol, etc . . . (daw)

The words are to be found on broadsides by Catnach, entitled 'The Beverley Maid and the Tinker', and the town is known as Beverley Town; by Swindells of Manchester ('The Tinker's Frolic'), by Harkness of Preston ('The Tinker and the Chambermaid'). Baring-Gould found the ballad coarse and Fleetwood Shepherd rewrote it for Songs of the West. *His version is amusing and witty but the words here given are the original.*

In Bodmin Town

Taken down from William Nicholls aged 68, in 1891.

1. In Bod-min Town there lived a maid, My in-no-cent heart she had be-trayed, I ne'er was woun-ded so be-fore, And yet I love her more and more.

2. In Bodmin Town when I did pass,
    I saw my sweet maid through the glass,
   All dressed in ribbons bright and gay,
    She looked more fair than flowers in May.

3. In Bodmin street when we did meet,
    We joined hands with kisses sweet,
   I wring my hands with bitter cry,
    That maiden I must wed or die.

4. In Bodmin Town her father knew,
    That she loved me so fast and true,
  He locked her in a chamber high,
    That I to her might not come nigh.

5. [To Bodmin Town I came by day,
    To see my true love on her way,
  But ne'er did I her vision gain,
    I came and went each day in vain.]

6. To Bodmin Town I came at night,
    And to her door I hurried straight,
  Come down! come down! and let me in,
    Your own true love pulls at the pin.

7. From bed she rose and down she came,
    She ope'd the door and let me in,
  I'm glad to see you love, she cried,
    Since you have gone my father died.

8. [In Bodmin Town the bells did ring,
    For we were married in the Spring,
  I ne'er was happy so before,
    And still I love her more and more.]

Published in the Garland of Country Song *no XXXIII. Baring-Gould says that 'The melody has been seriously affected in its termination by Wesleyan hymnody, as is the case with a vast number of airs collected in Cornwall.' Verses 5 and 8 were forgotten by the singer and are supplied by me.* G.H.

I rode my little horse

Taken down from Edmund Fry, a thatcher, Lydford 1889, also from John Bennett, a labourer of Chagford, and John Hunt, a shepherd, Postbridge.

1. I rode my lit-tle horse from London town I came, I went in-to the coun-try, to seek my-self a dame, And if I find a pret-ty maid be sure I'll kiss her then I'll swear that I will marry her but nev-er tell her *when*, but nev-er tell her *when*, I'll swear that I will mar-ry her but nev-er tell her *when*.

2. I found a buxom widow with many tons of gold,
    I lived upon her fortune as long as it would hold.
   I borrowed pounds a hundred, be'strode my horse and then
    I swore that I would marry her but would not tell her when.

3. A vintner had a daughter, the Golden Sun his sign.
    I tarried at his tavern and drank up all his wine.
   I tapped his richest hogsheads, be'strode my horse and then
    I swore the maid I'd marry but would not tell him when.

4. The guineas are expended, the wine is also spent.
    The widow and the maiden, they languish and lament,
   And if they come to seek me I'll ' pack them back again,
    I'll promise them I'll marry them but will not tell them when.

Jinny Jan

Stanzas 1–4 sent by a Mr Webber who heard it sung on Christmas Eve at a farmhouse in Brampford Speke, 1864. Known in other parts of Devon, it is enacted by several parties. A version in Everlasting Circle, *p 167. To my mind there is no more remarkable specimen of the singing game than 'Jenny Jones'—through which prosaic title we can discern the tender 'Jeanne Ma Joie' that formed the base of it. The Scots still say Jenny Jo, 'Jo' being with them a term of endearment (eg 'John Anderson, my Jo!').*

1. Come to see Jin-ny, Jan? Jinny, Jan? Jin-ny, Jan? Come to see Jinny? Can
   Jin   ny is washing, is   washing, is washing, (O) Jin-ny is washing. You

I see her now? Morn-ing la-dies and gen-tle-men too!
can't see her now.

Morn-ing la-dies and gen-tle-men too. Come to see Jin-ny, Jan,

Jin-ny, Jan, Jin-ny, Jan, Come to see Jin-ny and can't see her now.

Alternative in E:-

```
6 E - - B7 - -  | E - - B7 - -  | E(or C#m) - - A(or F#m) - - |
8

|B7 - - E - -  :|| C#m - - F#m - - | B7 - - C#m - - |

|E - - A - -  | B7 - - E - - | E - - B7 - - |

|E - - B7 - -  | E - - A - - | B7 - - E - - ||
```

2. Come to see Jinny, Jan? Jinny, Jan? Jinny, Jan?
   Come to see Jinny?
      Can I see her now?
   Jinny is married, married, married, Jan,
   Jinny is married, and she's nought to you.
      Chorus: Morning, ladies and gentlemen too,
      Morning, ladies and gentlemen too
      Come to see Jinny, Jan? Jinny, Jan? Jinny, Jan?
      Come to see Jinny and can't see her now.

3. Come to see Jinny, Jan? Jinny, Jan? Jinny, Jan?
   Come to see Jinny?
      Can I see her now?
   Jinny's dead indeed, dead indeed, dead indeed,
   Jinny is dead indeed, I swear and vow.   *Chorus*

4. Come to see Jinny, Jan? Jinny, Jan? Jinny, Jan?
   Come to see Jinny?
      Can I see her now?
   Jinny is buried, buried, buried, Jan,
   Jinny is buried, to all our woe.   *Chorus*

5. Come to see Jinny, Jan? Jinny, Jan? Jinny, Jan?
   Come to see Jinny?
      Where lies she now?
   Jinny's grave is green, grave is green, grave is green,
   Jinny's grave is green with the tears that flow.   *Chorus*

Jolly Waggoner

Taken down from Jas. Olver, Launceston, 1889

1. When first I went a-waggoning, a waggoning did go, I filled my parents' hearts with grief, with sorrow and with woe, And many were the hardships too that I did undergo, So wo! my lads, sing wo! Drive on my lads hi ho! Who would not lead the happy life we jolly waggoners do.

last verse or ad lib.

And ev'ry lad shall take a lass and dance her on his knee,— Sing,

2. Upon a cold and stormy night
    When wetted to the skin,
   I bear it with contentment,
    Till I get to the inn.
   And then I'll sit a-drinking boys,
    With the landlord and his kin.
    Refrain: Sing Wo! my lads, etc.

3. Now summer is a-coming boys,
    What pleasures we shall see,
   The small birds are a-singing out,
    On every greenwood tree.
   The blackbirds and the thrushes too,
    Are whistling merrily. *Refrain*

4. Now Michaelmas is coming, boys,
    What pleasure we shall see,
   Like chaff before the wind, my boys,
    'Twill make the red gold flee.
   And every lad shall take his lass,
    And dance her on his knee. *Refrain*

It appeared in a Garland of Country Song *and in* English Folk Songs for Schools. *I have chosen a slightly different melody from the one given in the collections mentioned, and the alternative ending given here sounds very much like the shanty 'A Roving'.*

The Lark in the Morn

Taken down from Samuel Gilbert for 52 years landlord of the Falcon Inn, at Mawgen in Pyder, aged 81, 1891. Some of the stanzas were coarse and Gilbert either did not know them or did not choose to sing them. Broadside ballad by Watts, Lane End (68). Also by Paul at B.M. 12621, K4; vol.1: p.379.

1. As I was a-walking one morning in May, I heard a young damsel them words did she say, Of all the calling whatever they may be, No life is like the ploughboy's in the month of May.

In E minor

4/4 ⅞		Em	-	-	-		Bm	(D)	Em	-	
	Em	-	-	-		Bm	D	Em	-	
	G	C	G	-		Am	D7	G	-	
	Em	-	Bm	-		C	D	Em	.	

Alternative to above:-

4/4 ⅞		Em	-	-	-		B7	-	Em	-	
	Em	-	-	-		B7	-	Em	-	
	Em	-	-	-		Am	D7	G	B7	
	Em	-	-	Am		Em	B7	Em	.	‖

2. The ' lark in the morning awakes from her nest,
   And ' mounts the white air with the dew on her breast,
   O the ' lark and the plough-boy together can sing,
   And re'turn to her nest in the evening.

3. One ' morning she mounted so high, oh, so high,
   And ' looked around her, and at the dark sky,
   In the ' morning she was singing and thus was her lay,
   There is ' no life like the plough-boy's in the sweet month of May.

4. When his ' day's work is over that he hath to do,
   O ' then to a fair or a wake will he go,
   And ' there he will whistle and there he will sing,
   And ' then to his fair love a ribbon will bring.

5. Good ' luck to the plough-boys wherever they be,
   They will ' take a sweet maiden to sit on the knee,
   They'll drink the brown beer, they will whistle and sing,
   O the ' plough-boy's more happy than noble or king.

This song was a favourite throughout England and is always associated with tunes of exquisite beauty. The melodies sung in Yorkshire and Cornwall are almost always the same.

Lark in the Morning

Taken down from Samuel Gilbert, landlord at the Falcon, 1891. See page 70

1. The lark in the morn-ing A-wakes from her nest, And mounts the white air with dew on her breast, O the lark and the plough boy to-geth-er can sing And re-turn to her nest in the cov-er-ing.

This tune may be used as an alternative to 'Lark in the Morn' but begin at verse 2.

2. The ′ lark in the morning awakes from her nest,
    And ′ mounts the white air with the dew on her breast,
  O the ′ lark and the plough-boy together can sing,
    And re′turn to her nest in the evening.

3. One ′ morning she mounted so high, oh, so high,
    And ′ looked around her, and at the dark sky,
  In the ′ morning she was singing and thus was her lay,
    There is ′ no life like the plough-boy's in the sweet month of May.

4. When his ′ day's work is over that he hath to do,
    O ′ then to a fair or a wake will he go,
  And ′ there he will whistle and there he will sing,
    And ′ then to his fair love a ribbon will bring.

5. Good ′ luck to the plough-boys wherever they be,
    They will ′ take a sweet maiden to sit on the knee,
  They'll drink the brown beer, they will whistle and sing,
    O the ′ plough-boy's more happy than noble or king.

A Lying Tale

Taken down from Will Nankervill, at Merrivale Bridge, 1890

1. O when I was an infant young To London I did go, A-mong the French and Spaniards then my gal-lant-ry to show, And when I came to the East-ern shore I let my head hang down, I trip-ped o-ver banks and hills and nev-er touched the ground: Fol-de-lid-dle, id-dle-i-do, Fol-de-liddle id-dle-day.

2. So when I reached the eastern shore,
    I met a giant high,
His feet they fillèd up the street,
    His head it touched the sky,
He lookèd down on me with scorn,
    He bade me pass him by
[I firmly stood and blocked his path,
    and never moved, not I.]
    Refrain: Fol de liddle, etc.

3. He challenged me to dance and sing,
    to whistle and to pipe,
I played on every instrument
    and beat the giant quite,
He challenged me to jump a brook,
    he challenged me to run,
I beat him out of all his pride,
    and [killed] him when I'd done. *Refrain*

4. The people all admiring stood,
    to see what I had done,
They gave to me a salver bright
    it weighed a hundred ton.
I made myself a little box
    it was three acres square
I filled it up unto the top
    with my bright silver ware. *Refrain*

5. So when I went to London town,
    I travelled on an ox,
And in my breeches pocket I
    did put my little box
And when I reached the western shore,
    They kicked me out of door,
They would not trust me for a pint,
    because that I looked poor. *Refrain*

6. I bought myself a flock of sheep,
    I thought they all were wethers*
And some of them brought little lambs
    and some brought only feathers
Methinks they were the best of sheep
    to give such good increase,
For every time the moon was full
    They had two lambs apiece. *Refrain*

7. I had a little poodle-dog,
    a poodle-dog was he,
Wherever I did chance to go,
    that poodle followed me,
His tail was only ten yards long,
    his ears but twelve feet wide,
And round the world in half-a-day
    upon him I could ride. *Refrain*

8. I bought myself a coal-black hen
    Of her I took much care,
I sat her on a cockle shell,
    And she hatched out a hare,
The hare, she grew at such a pace,
    She soon was ten hands high,
Come, if you know a better joke,
    I'm sure you tell a lie.

* castrated rams.

Published by Baring-Gould in Songs of the West *at no 72, the title 'The Song of the Moor.' Baring-Gould says the words are a whole string of absurdities, quite unworthy of the air and wrote fresh words. See also R. Climsall.* The Jovial Broom Man *and Chappell (ed)* Roxburgh Ballads.

Maids at eighteen

Taken down very kindly by Mrs. Hockin, of Stoke Fleming

1. Maids at eigh-teen, maids at nineteen, maids at twen-ty mar-ry,

Here am I at twenty-five and can no long-er tar-ry: With a

hey down, der-ry der-ry down, Maid or wife a hap-py life she

leads whose heart is free from strife; Sing hey down derry down dee.

In C.

2/4	C c	-	|G7 g	- d	|C g	C e	|F	C
|G7 d	-	|C g	C c	|G7 d	G7 g	|C c	C g
|C(or Em)	Am)	|C(or Em)	Am)	|F	C e	|D7	G7
|C	-	|G7	-	|C	G7	|C	-	

For Key D use Capo at the 2nd fret, and play as in C.

2. Sister Kate is far too young,
   She's younger far than I am,
   She's had sweethearts by the score,
   She's forced to deny 'em.
   Refrain: With a hey down, derry derry down, etc.

3. Sister Bet has an ugly face,
   Besides she is misshapen,
   Before that she was seventeen,
   A bride too she'd been maden. *Refrain*

4. Before that she was nineteen years,
   She'd a son and daughter,
   Here am I at twenty-five,
   Never had an offer. *Refrain*

5. Tinker, tailor, soldier, sailor,
   [Come before my charms fade,]
   Come and woo me, come and sue me,
   Don't let me die an old maid. *Refrain*

Baring-Gould published this in the Garland of Country Song *omitting two stanzas which were imperfect and 'toned down the impatience of the singer for the married life'. I have restored the two stanzas and the original words. See also 'Don't Let Me Die an Old Maid', in* Marrow Bones.

Months of the Year

Taken down from J. Potter, Postbridge, 1888

1. First comes Jan-u-a-ry When the sun lies ve-ry low   I

see in the farmer's yard— The cat-tle feed on stro'; The

wea-ther be-ing so cold While the snow lies on the ground There

will be an-o-ther change of moon Be-fore— the year comes round.

*In C.

```
6/8 ⁊ |C - - - - - |C - - - - - |C(or G)- - - - |F - - - - |
              e
|C - - - - - |G7 - - - - - |C - - D7 - - |Dm7 - - G7 - - |
      d
|Em - - F - - |F - - G7 - - |Am - - - - - |Dm7 - - C - - |
                                                        e
|F - - - - - |C - - - - - |Dm7 - - G7 - - |C - - - - - ||
              e
```

*Use Capo

2. Next is Febru'ary, so early in the Spring;
   The ' farmer ploughs the furrows, the birds their nests begin,
   The ' little lambs are playing, alongside of their dams;
   I ' think upon the increase, and thank God for the same.

3. March is the ' next month, the coldest in the year,
    Pre ' pare we now for harvest, by brewing of strong beer,
    God ' grant that all who labour, may see the harvest come,
    And ' drink the ale we're brewing, and dance at harvest home.

4. April is the ' next month, so early in the morn,
    I ' saw the cheery farmer, a-sowing of his corn.
    The ' gallant team come after, a-smoothing of the land.
    May ' heaven the farmer prosper, whate'er he takes in hand.

5. In ' May I go a-'walking, to hear the sweet birds sing,
    Their ' note was so delightful, a-praising God their King.
    It ' cheers the heart to hear them, as I walk on my way.
    Each ' warbling their notes, as on the trees sit they.

6. So ' early in the ' morning, awakes the Summer sun,
    The ' month of June is come now, and Winter cold is done;
    The ' cuckoo is a fine bird, she whistles as she flies,
    And ' as she whistles 'cuckoo!', the bluer grow the skies.

7. Six ' months I now have ' named, the seventh is July.
    Come ' lads and lassies to the field, your valour for to try.
    The ' farmer says: 'My hearty boys, be all of one good mind,
    For ' night comes on, my hearty boys, make hay whilst the sun shines.'

8. August brings the ' harvest, the reapers now advance.
    With ' meat and liquor plentiful, the work won't stand much chance,
    The ' farmer says, 'Well done my boys, the day shall be your friend.
    Come ' let us drink and make good work, and so the harvest ends.'

9. By the ' middle of Sep'tember, the rake is laid aside,
    The ' horses wear the breeching, rich dressing to provide;
    To do all things in season, methinks it just and right,
    The Summer season's ended, and frosts begin at night.

10. Oc'tober is a ' Winter month, I hope you know it all,
    The ' trees will soon be naked, the leaves begin to fall,
    The ' frosts will cut them clean-off, and never more be seen,
    For ' robbed are the meadows, that were so gay and green.

11. The e'leventh month, Nov'ember, the nights are cold and long,
    We'll ' go unto the ale house, and spend our nights in song.
    We'll ' sit about the fire, we cider drink and all,
    We'll ' kiss the pretty maidens, and tell a merry tale.

12. De'cember is the ' last month, that I am going to mention.
    For ' I shall go no further, it is not my intention.
    To con'clude and to be merry boys! and be of right good cheer,
    I ' wish you a merry Christmas, and a Happy New Year.

O the sweet dreams of Nancy

Words taken down from Matthew Baker, 1889, who said he learned it when aged 10. The tune and also the words from Matthew Ford and James Olver. Also taken down by Miss Templar from the singing of harvesters in 1834

2. On ' yonder tall mountain,
    A ' castle doth stand,
It is ' built of white ivory,
    All ' above the black sand,
All of ' ivory builded
    And of ' diamonds bright,
All with ' gold it is guilded,
    And it ' shines in the night.

3. On ' yonder high moorland,
    The ' wild fowl do fly,
There is ' one fair among them,
    Soars than ' others more high,
My ' heart is an eagle
    With ' wings wide outspread,
It ' soareth and flyeth,
    In pur'suit of my maid.

The Owl

Mr. Bussell noted down the melody from James Olver, tanner, of Launceston, in 1889. Olver could not recall all of the words.

1. Of all the birds that ev-er I see, The owl is the fair-est in her de-gree. For all the day long she sits in a tree, And when the night com-eth, a-way flies she. To whit! To who! says she, To who! Cin-a-mon, gin-ger, nut megs and cloves, And bran-dy gave me my jol-ly red nose.

2. The ' lark in the morn as'cendeth on high
    And leaves the poor owl to sob and to sigh;
And all the day long, the owl is asleep,
    While little birds blithely are singing, cheep! cheep!
    Refrain: To-whit! To-who! says she, To-who!
    Cinnamon, ginger, etc.

3. There's ' many a brave bird that boasteth awhile,
    And proves himself great, let Providence smile,
Be hills and be valleys all covered with snow,
    The poor owl will shiver and mock with Ho! Ho!
    Refrain: To-whit! To-who! says she, To-who!
    Cinnamon, ginger, etc.

2. When the parents came to know
      That their daughter loved him so,
   Then they sent a gang and pressed him to the sea.
      And they made of him a tar,
   To be slain in bloody war,
      Of the simple ploughboy singing on the lea. (*bis*)

3. Then this lonely maiden bold,
      She did line her purse with gold,
   And from her father's house she then did quickly flee,
      Then in male attire she dressed
   With a star upon her breast,
      All to seek the simple ploughboy on the sea.

4. Then she marched o'er hill and plain,
      And she went through showers of rain,
   Till she came unto the brink of the blue sea,
      Saying, I am forever to rove,
   For the loss of my true love,
      So am I rewarded for my pain.

5. Now the first she did behold,
      O it was a sailor bold.
   'Have you seen my little ploughboy?' then cried she,
      'Who is just gone on the deep,
   They have pressed him to the fleet,
      He is sent unto the wars for to be slain.'

6. Then she went to the captain,
      And to him she made complain,
   'O a silly ploughboy's run away from me,'
      And the captain smiled and said:
   'Sir! you're a pretty maid,
      So the ploughboy I will give up unto thee.'

7. Then she pulled out a store,
      Of five hundred guineas and more,
   And she strewed them on the deck, did she.
      Then he took her by the hand,
   And she rowed him to the land,
      Where she wed the little ploughboy back from sea.

Broadside versions published by Fortey, Hodges, Taylor, etc are all very corrupt. The version from Masters is exactly as he sang it, and is but one instance of the superiority of the ballads handed down traditionally over those from the ballad-mongers employed by broadside publishers.

Poor old horse
Words and melody from Matthew Baker

2. O ' once I lay in stable warm, all on good straw and on hay,
　　When fields were green and flowery, and meadows all were gay,
　But now there no such living, that I can find at all,
　　I'm forced to munch the nettles as grow on the kennel wall.
　　　　Poor old horse, till I die.

3. O ' once I lay in stable, free from ' cold and winter storm,
　　But now have no such usage, to keep me well and warm,
　I'm forced to lie in the open field, in the cold winter wind,
　　And stay beside a prickly bush some shelter for to find.
　　　　Poor old horse, till I die.

4. My ' shoulders that were once so glossy and so round,
　　They now are very rotten, I'm not accounted sound,
　So now that I grow old, my teeth go to decay,
　　My master frowns upon me, and I often hear him say,
　　　　Poor old horse, let him die.

5. My ' shoes and my skin, the huntsman he doth crave,
　　My flesh and bones to the dogs I very freely give,
　For I have followed after them for many and many a mile,
　　O'er hedges and o'er ditches, and over gate and stile.
　　　　Poor old horse, must I die.

Rich Nobleman

Taken down from Jas. Masters, Broadstone, 1891
Words also from J. Masters

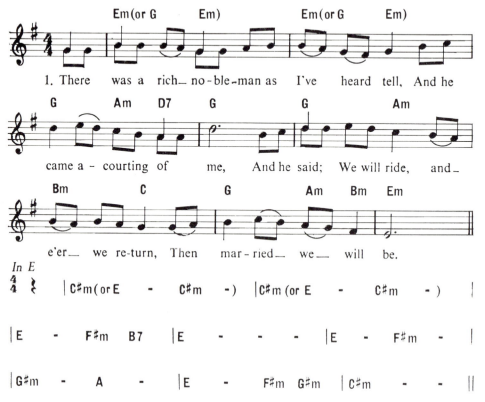

2. She ' went unto her ' father's stable,
   She was ' gay as gay might be,
   And she ' mounted upon her wild white steed,
   And the dapple grey rode he.

3. Jump ' off! Jump off! I pray he said,
   And de'liver your horse to me,
   Six ' pretty maids have ' I drowned here
   And the ' seventh thou shalt be.

4. Pull ' off, pull off, thy silken smock,
   And thy ' silken gown said he,
   Six ' pretty maids have ' I stripped here,
   And the ' seventh thou shalt be.

5. Take ' up the sickle and cut the nettle,
    That ' grows on the water brim,
  And she ' gave him a ' most cunning push,
    And she ' speedily pushed him in.

6. Lie ' there, lie there thou false-hearted knave,
    Lie ' there and drown said she,
  Six ' pretty maids hast ' thou drowned here,
    And the ' seventh drowneth thee.

7. And she ' mounted her on her milk-white steed,
    And she ' led the dapple grey,
  And she ' rode till she came to her father's hall,
    Just ' at the break of day.

8. O ' where have you been my fair, pretty queen,
    The ' parrot he did say,
  That ' you have been out all in the night,
    And re'turn before the day.

9. O ' hush and O hush! my pretty parrot,
    O ' say not a word, said she
  Thy ' cage it shall be of the beaten gold,
    That was ' of the timber tree.

10. Then ' up and spoke her father dear,
    From the ' bed whereon he lay,
  O ' what is the matter with my parrot,
    That he ' chatters before the day.

11. The ' cat came to my own cage door,
    And ' threatened to kill me,
  And I ' called aloud for help to come,
    To ' come and deliver me.

12. Well ' turned, well turned my pretty parrot,
    Well ' turned, well turned said she,
  Thy ' cage shall be made of the shining gold,
    That was ' of the timber tree.

Variously known as 'The False-hearted Knight'; 'The Outlandish Knight'; 'Lady Isabel and the Elf Knight', Child, Ballads no 4. The English versions have entirely lost their supernatural element as indicated in Child's title. The mode of trickery varies.

Rosemary Lane

Melody taken down from an old moor man by W. Crossing, Roger Luxton and Jas. Parsons also sang the same air

1. I served my app-ren-tice in Rose-mar-y Lane, And kept the good-will of my mas-ter and dame, A sail-or came by, With me want-ed to lie, And thus it be-gan all my mis-er-y.

2. The sailor was drowsy and hung down his head,
   He asked for a candle to light him to bed,
       I led him thereto
       As another might do,
   Said he: Pretty maid come my bed now into.

3. A silly young maiden, I thought it no harm,
   To lie in his bed and keep his back warm,
       But what happened there,
       I'll never declare,
   I would that short night [were] lasted seven year.

4. Next morning the sailor so early arose,
   And into my apron three guineas he throws,
       Saying take of my store,
       Aye, five and six more,
   A thousand times I that 'tis over deplore.

5. And if it's a girl she shall sit at her ease,
   And if it's a boy he shall cross the salt seas,
   　With his light little shoes,
   　And his ribbons and bows,
   And climb the high rigging when loud the wind blows.

Baring-Gould considered these words objectionable and published a version with words of his own see 'The Blue Flame', no 67 in Songs of the West. *Sharp and Hammond noted versions and the words have appeared on a broadside by Jackson of Birmingham. The refrain 'The Oak and the Ash' became attached to it and the song was known under this name.*

Roving Journeyman

Taken down from Jas. Parsons, 1888

1. O, I'm a rov-ing journ-ey-man I roam from town to town,— Where 'er I get a job of work I'm will-ing to sit down, With my kit up-on my shoul-der, And a graft-ing tool in hand,— So round the coun-try we will go, A-rov-ing journey-man.— *or end thus:* a rov-ing journ-ey-man.—

In A minor

6/8 ⁊	Am -	Am -	Em -
|Am -	Am -	Dm -	Dm -
|Am -	Am -	Dm -	Am -
|Em -	Am -	Am -	Em -
	A - ‖	Em -	A - ‖

For C minor use Capo at the 3rd fret

2. And when I came to Exeter
      The maidens jumped for joy,
   Said one unto another maid,
      Here comes a gallant boy.
   One treats me to a bottle,
      Another to a dram,
   And so the toast goes round, my boys,
      Here's a health to the journeyman.

3. I had not been in Exeter,
      The days were not full three,
   Before the mayor's daughter,
      She fell in love with me,
   She asked of me to dine with her,
      She took me by the hand
   She plainly told her mother that,
      She loved a journeyman.

4. Now out on thee, thou silly jade,
      Such folly speak no more,
   How can you love a journeyman,
      You've never seen before,
   O mother sweet, I do entreat,
      I love him all I can,
   And round the country I will go,
      With this young journeyman.

5. He need no more to trudge a-foot,
      We'll travel coach and pair,
   And round the country we will go,
      And travel everywhere,
   And when we find a job of work,
      We'll sit down where we can,
   So let the toast go round my boys,
      Here's a health to the journeyman.

Also taken down from William Aggett, Chagford. An inferior version of the words is to be found on broadsides by Catnach (see British Museum collection of broadsides, vol VII, 1162 L).

2. SHE: You are ragged, you are dirty,
    smell of tar.
    Get you gone to foreign countries
    from me far.
 HE: If I'm ragged, if I'm dirty,
    of tar I smell,
    Yet there's silver in my pocket,
    And of gold a store as well.

3. BOTH: When she saw the shining silver,
    saw the gold,
    Down she kneeled and very humbly
    hands did fold,
    Staying, she did hear these words
    on her knees she fell,
 SHE: Saying O forgive me love,
    For I like a sailor well.

4. HE: Do you think that I am maz'd,
    that I am mad,
    Wed ' a maiden ' where no fortune's
    to be had?*
    I will cross the raging ocean, or
    meadows green,
    Since you have re'fused my offer,
    An'other maid shall ' wear my ring.

*Original runs, 'For to wed a country maiden where no fortune's to be had.'

The ballad is frequent on broadsides by Disley, Pitts, Such and Hodges.

So deep in Love

Taken down by Rev. S. M. Walker of Saint Enoder, Cornwall from a very old man in his parish. Also from Sally Satterley at Huckaby Bridge, Dartmoor. A version in "Marrow Bones" says this may have originated from fragments of the 17th century ballad "Lord James Douglas".

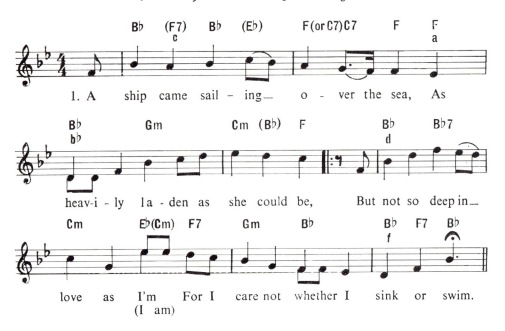

2. I leaned my back against an oak,
   Thinks I, I've found a trusty tree,
   But first it bent and then it broke,
   And ' so did my false love to me.

3. I put my hand into a bush,
   I thought a lovely rose to find,
   I pricked my finger to the bone,
   And left the lovely rose behind.

4. I wish! I wish! but 'tis in vain,
      I wish I had my heart again,
   I'd lock it in a golden box,
      I'd fasten it with a silver chain.

Sweet Nightingale

Taken down from the singing of four Cornish miners, 1854

2. Pretty Betty, don't fail,
    For I'll carry your pail
 Safe home to your cot as we go;
    You shall hear the fond tale
 Of the sweet nightingale,
    As she sings in the valleys below.

3. Pray let me alone,
    I have hands of my own,
 Along with you, sir, I'll not go,
    To hear the fond tale
 Of the sweet nightingale,
    As she sings in the valleys below.

4. Pray sit yourself down
    With me on the ground,
 On this bank where the primroses grow,
    You shall hear the fond tale
 Of the sweet nightingale,
    As she sings in the valleys below.

5. The couple agreed,
    And were married with speed,
 And soon to the church they did go;
    No more is she afraid
 For to walk in the shade,
    Nor to sit in those valleys below.

The air was sent to Baring-Gould by E. F. Stevens of The Terrace, St Ives, who said that 'the tune had been running in his head these eight and thirty years'. Baring-Gould obtained the song from many men in Cornwall, and always to the same air. The words are printed by Robert Bell in Ballads and Songs of the Peasantry of England *in 1857 who heard the song sung by four Cornish miners in Germany three years earlier. See also* Canow Kernow *(1966) where a three-part version is given with folk harmony.*

2. If a gentleman call,
  That his horse he may shoe,
 He will ' make no denial
  To one pot or two
 For to make his bright hammer, etc.

3. Here's a health to the fair maid,
  The maid he loves best,
 For she ' kindles a fire
  That doth ' burn in his breast
 And to make his bright hammer, etc.

4. Here's a health to King George,
  And a health to the Queen,
 Here is to the Royal Family
  Whenever they're seen,
 And to make his bright hammer, etc.

On 17 March when Alfred was King, he called together the Seven trades and declared his intention of making that tradesman king of all the trades who could get on best without the help of the others. Each was to bring a specimen of his work. The blacksmith brought a hammer and horseshoe. The tailor brought a new coat, the baker his peel and a loaf, the shoemaker an awl, the carpenter his saw, the butcher his chopper, the mason his chisel. The tailor's coat was so fine that the king pronounced the tailor king of all trades. The blacksmith was very angry and went away and threw away his tools. Now the king wanted his horse shoeing and one trade after another ran short of tools. So all came to the forge on 23 November (St Clement's Day) but no blacksmith was there. So they broke open the shop and each tried to do what he wanted—the king to shoe his horse, the baker to mend his peel, the butcher to sharpen his chopper, the mason to point his chisel. But the horse kicked, the fire would not burn and all began knocking each other about. Then in came St Clement with the blacksmith on his arm and the blacksmith shod the horse, pointed the chisel, mended the peel, sharpened the chopper, etc. Then the king made him prince and from that day this has been the blacksmith's song. This story was taken down in 1883 by E. Young from a poor fellow of Steyning in deep decline.

Twelve days of Christmas

M.S. by my aunt, Cecily Baring-Gould, about 1840. (B.G.)

3. Three French Hens, two turtle doves, and a part of a juniper tree.
4. Four Colley-birds, etc.
5. Five, a golden ring, etc.
6. Six geese a-laying, etc.
7. Seven swans a-swimming, etc.
8. Eight hares a-running, etc.
9. Nine ladies dancing, etc.
10. Ten lords a-playing, etc.
11. Eleven bears a-baiting, etc.
12. Twelve bulls a-roaring, etc.

The twelve days are, of course, those between Christmas Day and Epiphany. This cumulative song was a favourite among children in Devon where it is called the Nawden Song. The giving of forfeits was customary by those who could not remember the list of gifts. For other versions see Chambers's Popular Songs of Scotland, *Halliwell's* Nursery Rhymes *and* Northumbrian Minstrelsy. *The list of gifts varies and the last line of each rhyme is variously 'A part of a juniper tree'; 'A partridge in a pear tree.' There are also French and Languedoc versions of the song.*

Partridge, in common with many other speckled birds, was an emblem of the evil one. Pear tree has some magical properties associated with Christmas eve, although pear tree—perdrix (pertriz) in the French version—carried into the English language may have sounded like pear tree, 'joli perdrix' is a 'pretty juniper' or 'part of a juniper tree'.

Two turtle doves obviously has some reference to the 'true loves'. Having started with birds, thereafter birds were variously listed.

French Hens may simply mean rare (or foreign) fowl.

Colley-birds are blackbirds.

Gold rings—it seems likely that as this comes among the list of birds it may mean 'goldspinks' which are goldfinches.

Geese a-laying —common to all versions.

Swans a-swimming (steers a-running).

Hares a-running (swans a-swimming; deers a-running), etc.

Ladies dancing (drummers drumming; lords a-leaping).

Lords a-playing (pipers piping; ladies dancing; bells a-ringing).

Bears a-baiting (ladies dancing; bulls a-bleating).

Bulls a-roaring (lords a-leaping; cocks a-crowing; bells a-ringing; ships a-sailing).

For fuller accounts see Folk Song Journal, *20 p 280. See also 'The Jolly Gosshawk' which runs: 'I went to my lady the first day of May.'*

Further notes occur in The Folk Carol of England, *p 88.*

The best-known version of this is the setting by Richard Austin who inserted music for the phrase 'five gold rings'.

2. Now ' for this good liquor to us, that you bring,
    We ' lift up our voices we merrily sing,
   That ' all good householders may continue still,
    To pro'vide the brown liquor, our bowl for to fill.
   Refrain: With ' our wassail! wassail! wassail!
   And ' joy come to our jolly wassail!

3. We ' wish you great plenty and long may you live,
    Be'cause you are willing and free for to give,
   To ' our wassail so cheerful, our wassail [so] bold,
    Long ' may you live happy, and lusty, and old. *Refrain*

4. Now ' neighbours and strangers you ever shall find,
    The ' wassailers courteous, obliging and kind,
   We ' hope our civility you will approve,
    With a ' piece of small silver in token of love. *Refrain*

5. O ' welcome, kind Sir, as we merrily meet,
    With ' our jolly wassail as we pass up the street,
   O ' welcome, kind Sir, if it please you to stop,
    A ' piece of small silver in our bowl for to drop. *Refrain*

6. Now ' jolly old Christmas is passing away,
    He's ' posting off fancies and this the last day,
   That ' we shall enjoy long o' you to abide,
    So ' farewell, old Christmas, a merry good tide. *Refrain*

7. Now ' jolly old Christmas thou welcomest guest,
    Then ' from us art parting, which makes us look
   For ' all the twelve days are now come to an end,
    And ' this the last day of the season we spend. *Refrain*

8. Now ' for this good liquor, your cider, your beer,
    And ' for the fair kindness that we have had here,
   We re'turn you our thanks and shall still bear in mind,
    How ' you have been bountiful, lovely and kind. *Refrain*

9. Now ' for the great kindness that we did receive,
    We re'turn you our thanks and we take now our leave,
   From ' this present evening we bid you adieu!
    Un'til the next year and same season ensue. *Refrain*

Verse 5 is sung on meeting any stranger whilst going round from house to house.

Widdecombe Fair

Taken down from W. F. Collier, Woodtown, 1888

1. "Tom Pearce, Tom Pearce, lend me your grey mare, All along down along.

out along, lee, For I want for to go — to Widdecombe Fair, Wi' Bill

Brewer, Jan Stewer, Peter Gurney, Peter Davy, Dan'l Whiddon, Harry Hawk, old

Uncle Tom Cobbley and all, — old Uncle Tom Cobbley and all." —

    2. 'And when shall I see again my grey mare?'
        All along, etc.
      'By Friday soon, or Saturday noon,
        Wi' Bill Brewer, etc.

    3. Then Friday came, and Saturday noon,
        All along, etc.
      But Tom Pearce's old mare hath not trotted home
        Wi' Bill Brewer, etc.

    4. So Tom Pearce he got up to the top o' the hill
        All along, etc.
      And he seed his old mare down a-making her will
        Wi' Bill Brewer, etc.

    5. And how did he know it was his grey mare?
        All along, etc.
      'Cos one foot was shod and the other was bare.
        Wi' Bill Brewer, etc.

6. So Tom Pearce's old mare, her took sick and died.
    All along, etc.
  And Tom he sat down on a stone, and he cried
    Wi' Bill Brewer, etc.

7. And now that Tom Pearce's old grey mare is dead,
    All along, etc.
  They all agreed that her should be buried
    Wi' Bill Brewer, etc.

8. But this isn't the end o' this shocking affair,
    All along, etc.
  Nor, though they be dead, of the horrid career
    Of Bill Brewer, etc.

9. When the wind whistles cold on the moor of a night
    All along, etc.
  Tom Pearce's old mare doth appear, gashly white,
    Wi' Bill Brewer, etc.

10. And all the long night be heard skirling and groans,
    All along, etc.
  From Tom Pearce's old mare in her rattling bones,
    And from Bill Brewer, Jan Stewer, Peter Gurney,
    Peter Davy, Dan'l Whiddon,
    Harry Hawk, old Uncle Tom Cobbley and all.
    Chorus   Old Uncle Tom Cobbley and all.

Certainly the best-known and most popular of all Devonshire airs. An older form of the melody is given in the MS. The original 'Uncle Tom Cobley' lived in a house near Yeoford Junction in the parish of Spreyton. The names in the chorus were all residents of Sticklepath. Printed in Songs of the West *with verse 5 omitted. Cecil Sharp noted a version 'Midsummer Fair' in Somerset. Sometimes the words ended with a jingle instead of names.*

The Wreck off Scilly

Words and music from James Parsons

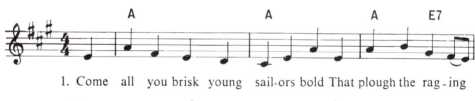

1. Come all you brisk young sail-ors bold That plough the rag-ing

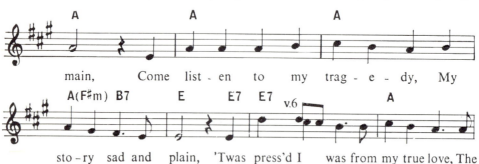

main, Come list-en to my trag-e-dy, My sto-ry sad and plain, 'Twas press'd I was from my true love, The

gal-lant ships to steer, To In-dies West each

heart beat high, With con-fi-dence and cheer.

At bar 6 the following seems easier:-

My sto-ry sad and plain

    2. Sometimes alone I make my moan,
        While others laughter make,
    I think of my true love all day,
        I'm sad for her dear sake.
    Sometimes on deck, sometimes aloft,
        And oftentimes below,
    The thought of her is in my heart,
        When stormy winds do blow.

3. A year was gone and home at last,
    We turned with swelling sail,
  When we o'er [the] Scilly over-past,
    There broke on us a gale.
  The boatswain up aloft did go,
    He went aloft so high,
  He looked around on every side,
    Nor land nor light could spy.

4. To make the stripe in vain we tried,
    The Scilly rocks to clear,
  On ocean wide we must abide,
    Till daylight did appear.
  There came a sharp and sudden shock
    Then loud the captain cried,
  The Lord have mercy on us all
    And on our wives betide.

5. Of eighty seamen in the crew,
    But one did reach the shore,
  Our gallant ship to pieces went,
    That was so good before.
  And when the news to Plymouth came,
    That our good ship was gone,
  Then wet with tears was many an eye,
    And many a wife forlorn.

6. And when to Plymouth I did come,
    Alone of eighty lost,
  Then many a sailor's heart did fear
    The danger of that coast.
  My own Polly love you must lament,
    The loss of your sweetheart,
  The angry seas and stormy winds,
    Caused you and me to part.

This is one of the favourite 'Come all ye's' type of ballad. Eleven verses noted by Hammond in 'Scilly Rocks' and six verses noted by Walter Ford, see Folk Song Journal *no 19, pp 171–3. These rocks have been a menace to shipping over the ages, not least of all in the recent tragedy of the* Torrey Canyon, *which spilled her oil-slick over many miles along the coasts of Britain and France, killing thousands of birds and much marine life.*

Sabine Baring-Gould

Parson, Squire, Novelist, Hymn-writer, Antiquarian, Pioneer Folk-Song Collector

A memoir by his grandson, Bickford H. C. Dickinson

SABINE BARING-GOULD grew up to a life of genteel vagabondage. Each year his parents and their family would spend the winter in some favoured spot on the continent within easy reach of the English mail. This was vitally important as his father was a great reader and expected to receive regularly each monthly instalment of Mr Charles Dickens's latest novel.

Each spring they would move on again. Sometimes they journeyed down ancient highways, making their sedate progress down roads that had felt the tread of Roman legions. At other times the ironbound wheels of their carriage rolled smoothly along military roads of Napoleon's creation. Yet again they would jolt and sway along deeply rutted tracks, when Mrs Baring-Gould would suffer, uncomplaining, agonies of discomfort. Then at last they would pause a while: a month; three months, for time was no object; and then on again. So it came about that during the most formative years of his life, Sabine never had any place that he could call home; never had the mental discipline of regular schooling; and never learned to play one outdoor game. Set against this, he had an unique opportunity to develop his natural love of beauty and by the age of fifteen he could speak five languages fluently.

In 1851, the Baring-Goulds at last returned home and for a while settled in the market town of Tavistock on the edge of Dartmoor.

For one happy, carefree summer the boy Sabine, then aged seventeen, wandered over the moor, his long legs astride a shaggy Dartmoor pony, and during these months two of the main interests of his life, for which he will be long remembered, were formed. By day he gazed and wondered at the countless megalithic survivals of bygone men which studded the moor and in the evenings he sat enchanted in the corner of some wayside inn and listened to the old moormen singing the traditional folk-songs that in years to come he was to be the first to record.

In the following year he entered Clare Hall, Cambridge, as a Classical student. While at the university he read enormously, storing away a mass of curious information which was to serve him well in later life as a writer, but he was handicapped by his lack of regular early schooling and only obtained a pass degree. It was while he was at Cambridge that his religious convictions crystallised and he left the university a devout and enthusiastic High Churchman.

From Cambridge he went as an unpaid voluntary teacher to the Choir School of St Barnabas, Pimlico, and from there to Lancing and then to Hurstpierpoint School, where he remained until his ordination in 1864, drawing a salary which began at £25 and finally rose to £40 a year.

After his ordination by Robert Bickersteth, the Evangelical Bishop of Ripon, he at once went to serve as assistant curate in the town of Horbury in Yorkshire. Fortunately for him the Rector, the Rev John Sharp, was a remarkable man, who had the good sense to realise that in Sabine he had an experienced schoolmaster, used to responsibility, who was not only capable of working alone but was temperamentally best suited to do so.

While at Horbury he wrote the hymns which were to make him famous: 'Through the Night of Doubt and Sorrow', 'Now the Day is Over', 'On the Resurrection Morning' and 'Onward, Christian Soldiers'.

Circumstances, however, forced him to move from Horbury. An intellectual, dedicated man of over thirty, he fell madly in love with a sweet but completely uneducated mill girl of sixteen. Against all opposition he had her educated at his own expense and in 1867 he moved to the minute parish of Dalton, marrying her in the following year. His father died in 1871 and, as eldest son, he was now squire of Lew Trenchard but it was not until his uncle Charles, who for many years had been rector of Lew Trenchard, had also died that he presented himself to the family living and returned to Devon as squire and parson.

Few men have been able to start a new life successfully at forty-seven and fewer havé had the chance to carry it on under almost ideal conditions as Sabine did for another forty-three years. He set himself three tasks; the much-needed spiritual rousing of the people of the parish; the rebuilding of his home and the repair of the farms and cottages on the estate; and the restoration of the parish church; at all of which he laboured untiringly for the remainder of his life. Both his home and his church still bear about them the unmistakable marks of his strong and unusual personality. Neither are quite English, for he was, thanks to his early upbringing, more cosmopolitan than English. He ransacked all Europe to make his church beautiful. The screen was rebuilt to conform with an ancient picture of what had been there before it had been swept away in 1832; the lectern was saved from a church in Brittany, the fifteenth-century chandelier from Belgium. In the same way his house is a remarkable amalgam of German, French and English stonework and wood-carving, yet somehow it is redolent of the personality of a man who loved beautiful things wherever he found them and had the power to combine them into a pleasing whole.

His interests were innumerable and his curiosity insatiable. He was among the first to establish the fact that the huge standing stones on Dartmoor were not the work of the Druids, as had been formerly believed, but the memorials of the men of the Bronze Age. He fought gallantly, at times fiercely, for the preservation of the ancient landmarks, which in his time were being almost everywhere uprooted and defaced. He strove to preserve and restore all the beauty and dignity of Catholic worship which the Reformation had so nearly destroyed in the Church of England. He was the champion of all that was beautiful and worthy of preservation in the work of former generations.

It was this that led him in 1888 to start what was to be perhaps his greatest task; the collection of the traditional folk-songs of the West of England.

He was handicapped by the fact that he was not a trained musician and could only take down, note by note upon a piano, the tunes as he received them; and he was even then only just in time, as some of the old singers were already dead and others senile. He succeeded however in visiting or entertaining at his house over sixty of them and recording their songs. For the music he depended upon two friends. One was Mr F. W. Bussell, Doctor of Music and Fellow of Brasenose College, Oxford, and the other was the Rev H. Fleetwood Sheppard, a recognised authority on sacred music, especially plain-song. With them he journeyed hundreds of miles in his dog-cart, by train and on foot across Devon and Cornwall, recording songs which otherwise would undoubtedly have been lost for ever.

The resulting *Songs of the West* was first published in four parts in 1889, fifteen years before Cecil Sharp's *Folk Songs of Somerset*.

In 1890, Sabine went still further in his desire to make the songs better known. At his own expense he organised a tour of the leading towns in Devon and Cornwall, personally leading a concert party which gave programmes of solos, duets, choruses, tableaux and dances, all in costume.

It was not until his wife died in 1916 that his energy began to abate and he became almost overnight a very old man. Though he continued to write the fire went out of his work and it tended to become more and more disjointed. Yet he lingered on for another eight years, his sight, hearing and vigour steadily deteriorating. His end, when at last it came in January 1924, was peaceful. They laid him to rest beside his wife in Lew Trenchard Churchyard and at the graveside they sang his children's hymn 'Now the Day is Over'.

His day was indeed over. He had outlived it by a decade, for the world he knew, loved and understood had changed for ever with the outbreak of the Great War.

Reprinted from *English Song and Dance* by permission of the English Folk Dance and Song Society.

L